Children of the World
Guatemala

972.8105
CUM

9/95
15.95

For a free color catalog describing Gareth Stevens' list of high-quality children's books, call 1-800-341-3569 (USA) or 1-800-461-9120 (Canada).

For their help in the preparation of *Children of the World: Guatemala*, the writer and editors gratefully thank: Patricia Mendoza, First Secretary, Embassy of Guatemala, Washington, DC; Professor Rosa Helena Chinchilla, University of Wisconsin-Milwaukee; Professor Michael Fleet, Marquette University, Milwaukee; and Professor Howard Handelman, University of Wisconsin-Milwaukee.

Flag illustration on page 48, © Flag Research Center.

Library of Congress Cataloging-in-Publication Data

Cummins, Ronald.
    Guatemala / written by Ronnie Cummins; photography by Rose Welch.
       p. cm. — (Children of the world)
    Includes bibliographical references.
    Summary: Presents the life of a young Mayan Indian girl in a Guatemalan lakeside village, describing her family, her day-to-day life, and the history, political system, and customs of her country.
    ISBN 0-8368-0120-2
    1. Guatemala—Social life and customs—Juvenile literature. 2. Children—Guatemala—Juvenile literature. [1. Family life—Guatemala. 2. Guatemala—Social life and customs.] I. Welch, Rose, ill. II. Title. III. Series: Children of the world (Milwaukee, Wis.)
    F1463.5.C86 1990   972.8105'3—dc20   89-40246

A Gareth Stevens Children's Books edition

Edited, designed, and produced by
Gareth Stevens Children's Books
RiverCenter Building, Suite 201
1555 North RiverCenter Drive
Milwaukee, Wisconsin 53212, USA

Series editor: Valerie Weber
Editor: Amy Bauman
Research editor: Scott Enk
Designer: Laurie Shock
Map design: Sheri Gibbs

Printed in the United States of America

   2 3 4 5 6 7 8 9 96 95 94 93 92 91 90

Children of the World
Guatemala

by Ronnie Cummins
Photography by Rose Welch

Gareth Stevens Children's Books
MILWAUKEE

. . . a note about *Children of the World*:

The children of the world live in fishing towns, Arctic regions, and urban centers, on islands and in mountain valleys, on sheep ranches and fruit farms. This series follows one child in each country through the pattern of his or her life. Candid photographs show the children with their families, at school, at play, and in their communities. The text describes the dreams of the children and, often through their own words, tells how they see themselves and their lives.

Each book also explores events that are unique to the country in which the child lives, including festivals, religious ceremonies, and national holidays. The *Children of the World* series does more than tell about foreign countries. It introduces the children of each country and shows readers what it is like to be a child in that country.

Children of the World includes the following published and soon-to-be-published titles:

Australia	El Salvador	Japan	Spain
Bhutan	England	Jordan	Sweden
Bolivia	Finland	Malaysia	Tanzania
Brazil	France	Mexico	Thailand
Burkina Faso	Greece	Nepal	Turkey
Burma	Guatemala	New Zealand	USSR
China	Hong Kong	Nicaragua	Vietnam
Costa Rica	Hungary	Philippines	West Germany
Cuba	India	Singapore	Yugoslavia
Czechoslovakia	Indonesia	South Africa	Zambia
Egypt	Italy	South Korea	

. . . and about *Guatemala*:

Maria, a Mayan Indian girl, lives in a village on Lake Atitlán. She is in the fourth grade and wants to become a teacher. She likes to draw and paint, and is learning traditional Mayan weaving from her mother. Like many Guatemalan children, she spends long hours doing household chores, but finds time to play with her friends.

To enhance this book's value in libraries and classrooms, comprehensive reference sections include up-to-date information about Guatemala's geography, demographics, language, currency, education, culture, industry, and natural resources. *Guatemala* also features a bibliography, research topics, activity projects, and discussions of such subjects as Guatemala City, the country's history, political system, ethnic and religious composition, and languages.

The living conditions and experiences of children in Guatemala vary tremendously according to economic, environmental, and ethnic circumstances. The reference sections help bring to life for young readers the diversity and richness of the culture and heritage of Guatemala. Of particular interest are discussions of the traditional ways of the Mayan Indians from the Spanish conquest to modern times, the role of religion in their lives, and how they maintain their cultural identity in the face of modern economics and politics.

CONTENTS

Maria, third from left, stands with (from left) her father, Diego, her brother, Pedro, and her mother, who is also named Maria, behind their Santiago Atitlán home.

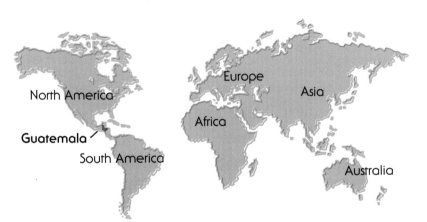

North America

Guatemala

South America

Europe

Africa

Asia

Australia

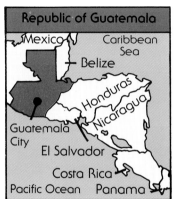

Republic of Guatemala

Mexico

Caribbean Sea

Belize

Honduras

Nicaragua

Guatemala City

El Salvador

Costa Rica

Pacific Ocean

Panama

6

LIVING IN GUATEMALA:
Maria, a Girl from Lake Atitlán

Guatemala is home to 12-year-old Maria de los Angeles Reanda. Maria, who belongs to a Mayan Indian tribe called the Tzutuhils, lives in the town of Santiago Atitlán with her parents and her older brother, Pedro. In Santiago Atitlán, about 95% of the people are Indians. The remainder of the townspeople are Ladinos, which means they have a mixture of Indian and Spanish blood.

Santiago Atitlán, a town of 25,000 people, lies on the south-western shore of Lake Atitlán, Guatemala's second largest lake. The town sits at the base of three large volcanoes. Many visitors to Guatemala have traveled to Maria's village to see Lake Atitlán. They say that this lake is one of the most beautiful, colorful bodies of water in the world.

Towering volcanoes surround Lake Atitlán. The lake, with its beautiful blue water, is said to be over 1,000 feet (300 m) deep.

Santiago Atitlán crowds the shore of Lake Atitlán. The San Pedro volcano rises in the background.

The simple Reanda house stands on a hill, overlooking the rest of its street.

At Home on the Lake

Legends and stories of ancient Guatemala fascinate Maria. One of her favorite legends explains how Lake Atitlán came to be. As the legend has it, Jesus' apostles once passed through Guatemala. Tired from walking, they stopped to eat lunch and rest. "How sad it is that there is no water here," said Saint James. He then dug a large hole in the ground and threw in the drinking water that was left over from their lunch. The pool of water grew until it became beautiful Lake Atitlán.

Maria's town was named Santiago (which is Spanish for "Saint James") in honor of this apostle. Many of Maria's aunts, uncles, and cousins live here. Their houses are close enough so that Maria can visit with her cousins after school. Other relatives live in the village of San Pedro — an hour's journey by canoe.

◀ Maria proudly shows off Canela, her new puppy.

Maria loves the one-room house with the walled-in backyard that she and her family call home. Her mother's family built it over 100 years ago. Like traditional Tzutuhil houses, the Reanda house is made of heavy stone blocks covered by white plaster. Maria's relatives dug these stones from the lake's shoreline and from the volcano's lower slopes. They then carved the stones to fit together so that a small amount of clay or mortar would hold them in place.

Few houses in Santiago Atitlán have indoor plumbing. Like the Reandas, most families use outdoor toilets, or outhouses. For drinking and cooking, Maria and her family carry water from the lake, where they also bathe. Sometimes, however, they take steam baths in the wood-heated sauna in their backyard. Maria prefers a steam bath to a bath in the lake, which can sometimes be very cold. Very few houses have electricity either, but Maria's house has a single light bulb in the kitchen.

Opposite page: Maria fills a water jug on one of her many daily trips to the lake. Below: A back view of the Reanda house is seen against a close-up of the stone wall that encloses the backyard.

JOHNSBURG JR. HIGH SCHOOL

13

Morning at the Reandas' House

The Reandas' day starts before sunrise. Rising at 4:30 a.m., Maria and her mother begin preparing breakfast. Meanwhile, Pedro and Diego collect firewood, fish in the lake, or gather beans or corn from the garden. Although the family has much to do even at this hour, no one hurries. Everyone seems to appreciate the quiet of the early morning.

Maria lights a fire to heat their breakfast of black beans, tortillas, and coffee. Then she carries a bowl of corn — which her mother has soaked overnight in lime and water — to the village *molino,* or corn grinder. The molino grinds the corn into a paste that the women use to make the round, flat tortillas. Walking back toward the house, Maria hears music. As he often does, Diego is playing a tune on his recorder before breakfast. Maria loves the soothing sound, and he is pleased to play for her.

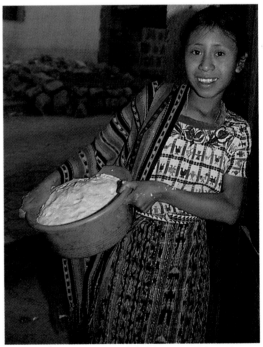

Top: Before sunrise, women and girls from all over the village flock to the building that houses the molino.
Bottom: The sun has yet to rise as Maria returns to the house carrying a bowl of ground corn paste, called *masa.*

Top: Maria's mother demonstrates the proper way to knead dough.
Left: The music from Diego's recorder glides on the early-morning stillness.
Right: Maria offers a tiny bit of her breakfast to one of the rabbits in the backyard.

15

A Short School Day

Maria's school, Mateo Herrera Elementary School, has 500 students in grades one through six. Maria is in the fourth grade, but her classmates are from both the fourth and fifth grades. The school year begins in January and ends in October, and classes last four hours per day. Maria's classes run from nine in the morning until one in the afternoon.

Maria is eager to go to school and see all her friends. She studies very hard because someday she wants to become a schoolteacher. Several village girls have received scholarships to attend high school and teachers' training school outside Santiago Atitlán. Maria hopes to earn a scholarship, too. Today, Maria can't wait to finish her math, reading, writing, and science classes so she can go to art, which is her favorite class. She even wishes that recess wouldn't take so long.

Some days, when she'd rather be out playing or drawing with Pedro, Maria must try hard to keep her mind on her lessons.

Above: Maria's fourth- and fifth-grade class lines up in front of Mateo Herrera Elementary School. The school is small, simple, and — like many other Guatemalan schools — overcrowded.
Left: Maria's classmate looks up from his work of copying the day's lesson into his notebook.

Above insets and background: Recess has moments of wild play as well as those of quiet conversation.

Above inset: Maria's pens, notebooks, and schoolbooks are spread out beside the book bag that Pedro embroidered for her.

At recess and sometimes after school, Maria joins the other children for games and sports. Maria's favorite sport is basketball, and she and her friends play almost every day on the basketball court behind the school. Pedro and some of the other boys spend most of their time playing soccer. Soccer is the most popular sport in Guatemala as it is throughout most of Latin America.

When it's time for classes again, the teacher often has a lesson on the board for the children to copy. Because Guatemala's government provides little money for education, Maria's school cannot afford textbooks, so the students must copy each lesson into their notebooks. Maria does not mind the extra work. She thinks the school is fortunate just to have a teacher.

The political turmoil that has plagued Guatemala since 1954 has caused many such problems. As the country's government and rebel groups repeatedly clash, the violence affects life throughout the country. Some teachers are afraid to take jobs in areas where clashes have occurred.

Opposite page: At snack time, a group of boys crowd around the snack table,
each trying to wiggle his way to the front.
Above: Diego and Maria share an interest in books and education.

Diego has told Maria and Pedro that about half of Guatemala's
adults cannot read or write. Maria knows many people in
Santiago Atitlán who would like to go to school. But many, like
Maria's father, are not able to attend because they must work
to support their families. Diego learned to read and write on
his own, but he wants a better education for his children. He
believes that a solid education can mean a better life, so he
encourages Maria and Pedro to study hard. Maria does well, but
sometimes she'd rather play with friends than do her homework.

Maria and Pedro hope to attend classes beyond the sixth
grade. They know this means they will have to live away
from the village. Because many families cannot afford this, few
children from Santiago Atitlán complete high school. Already,
the Reanda family is saving money so that Pedro can go away
to a secondary school next year. If he can complete high school,
Pedro is less likely to be drafted into the army. Like Maria, he
wants to be a schoolteacher.

Maria's mother stands before the huge family stove, stirring a bowl of tomato sauce that she has been heating.

Never an Idle Moment for the Reandas

Everyone in Maria's family is used to working long hours. Usually, Maria and Pedro help their parents both before and after school. While Diego and Pedro work in the fields and fish on the lake, Maria and her mother work around the house.

As each Guatemalan mother has done for centuries, Maria's mother is teaching her all the traditional skills acquired by women. They work side by side, shaping tortillas, grinding tomato paste, scrubbing clothing at the lakeshore, or weaving colorful fabrics. With each task, Maria's mother patiently explains the details. Of all her chores, Maria thinks that feeding the rabbits and chickens in the backyard is the most fun. Weaving is the most difficult. When it is time to practice her weaving, Maria sometimes wishes she could hide.

Right: Maria's mother wraps tomato sauce in banana-tree leaves. Pedro and Diego will take sauce and tortillas with them when they go to work in the fields.
Below and bottom: Banana-tree leaves also serve as food for the animals. Maria climbs a tree to cut some leaves for the rabbits and chickens, who greedily nibble on them.

Maria tries to find fun in her work. She thinks even jobs such as hauling water and washing clothes have their good points since they give her time to visit with her friends Candelaria and Elena. While they work, the girls swap news of family, friends, and school. They talk while carrying water from the lake in jugs that they balance on their heads. To keep their families supplied with water, the girls have to make this trip several times each day. Then, before it is safe for her family to drink, Maria must boil the water.

Maria's mother takes great care with the family's clothing, always making sure it is spotless. This means that mother and daughter must make many trips to the lake, where they wash their clothes by hand. After lathering the clothes with soap, Maria uses a rock as a washboard, scrubbing until her fingers are sore. She then spreads the clean clothes in the sun, where they dry quickly.

◀ Standing in water over her knees, Maria scrubs the family wash against a huge rock. Below: Maria and Elena break from their chores long enough for a quick game of marbles. Since they only have one marble, the girls use bottle caps to mark the position of the other marbles. When the game is finished, the girls join Candelaria in filling the water jugs.

Canoes, called *cayucos*, are moored in a row awaiting the fishermen.
Maria's family has a canoe that looks like one of these.

Most of Maria's relatives are farmers, but her uncle Vinicio is a fisherman. Diego and Pedro work at both jobs to provide food for the family. On some days, they spend many hours fishing on Lake Atitlán, casting nets for carp or trout. On other days, they farm either their own land or help relatives in their fields in nearby San Pedro.

In the family garden and cornfield, the Reandas grow corn, beans, squash, tomatoes, cucumbers, and peppers. They also tend several orange and coffee trees. When the coffee beans ripen to red, the Reandas pick them from the tree and place them in the sun to dry. Later on, the beans will be roasted to produce the dark coffee beans that people recognize.

Top: Diego and Pedro weave reeds to
make a mat known as a *petate*. When
they are through weaving the mats, they
will dry them in the sun. Once the mats are
dry, family members will sleep on them.
Above: A close-up of the mat shows
the weaving pattern.
Right: Diego picks ripe coffee beans.

Above: A small boy harvests sugarcane on one of the local plantations.

During the rainy season, from May through October, the garden gets plenty of water. But during the dry months, Diego and Pedro must carry water from the lake to irrigate their plants. The Reandas are fortunate to own a plot of land only about 1 mile (2 km) outside of the village right on the lakeshore. Sometimes, Maria helps her father and brother in the fields.

Many villagers do not have enough land to feed their families, so they must buy some of their food. They earn extra money by working as laborers on nearby coffee, sugarcane, and cotton plantations. These plantations, owned by wealthy Guatemalans called *patrones*, are huge areas of cropland that need many hands to plant, weed, and harvest. Maria's father worked on a plantation as a boy. There he saw children as young as six years of age cutting sugarcane. Maria is happy that she and Pedro don't have to spend long hours cutting sugarcane or picking coffee beans on a plantation.

◀ Diego and Pedro harvest black beans from the garden. The narrow plot of land that the garden grows on has been in the Reanda family for generations.

Top: The orphanage has a thatched roof that is a traditional feature of Guatemalan buildings.
Left: These girls, pictured beneath a wood carving made by the orphans,
are two of the many neighborhood people who work for the orphanage.
Right: One of the many orphans peers shyly at the camera. The political violence
in Guatemala has orphaned thousands of children. Their number has grown so large
that Santiago Atitlán needs several orphanages.

Time Out for Maria

Although Maria has many responsibilities, she still finds time to have fun. After finishing her homework each day, she often visits with her cousin Juana and her friends Candelaria and Elena. Often, the girls walk to the lake, stopping at the orphanage that they pass along the way. Maria can't resist talking with the younger orphans; many have lost their parents in Guatemala's political fighting. While there, Maria also peeks in the weaving workshop that some of the village widows operate in a room in the orphanage. Maria thinks the weavings are quite beautiful but she is glad she doesn't have to do the weaving.

Today, Maria waits at home for Pedro. Although they have separate sets of friends at school, they do many things together and share many interests. Often, they spend the afternoons playing with Maria's puppy, Canela. If the lake is calm, they may go for a ride in the canoe. They may even take Canela along. Sometimes, they explore the forest, looking for unusual leaves. After supper, they try to identify each leaf before adding it to their collection. Diego helps them with leaves they don't recognize.

Pedro takes Maria for a ride in the family canoe.

One of Pedro's watercolors shows a ceremony in the temple of Maximón.

But most often, Maria and Pedro get out their watercolors and paint. Their simple paintings colorfully capture Guatemalan landscapes and scenes from Atitlán life. Several of their latest pictures portray Maximón, the god of the Tzutuhils. The children sell their watercolors and drawings to passing tourists. They put aside most of their earnings for school, but some of the money is used to buy new paint supplies.

In the evening, Maria and Pedro beg their father to tell them stories of the ancient Mayan people. The children are especially fascinated by the stories that describe how the Tzutuhils lived before the Spanish conquistadores came in the 1500s. Diego's stories are the same as those that his father and grandfather told him. Retelling family and village tales is one way that the Tzutuhils preserve their history and customs.

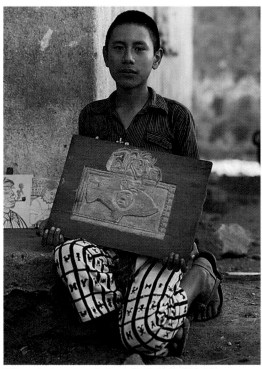

When he's not painting, Pedro spends time working on his wood carvings.

Maria puts finishing touches on one of her most recent paintings.

33

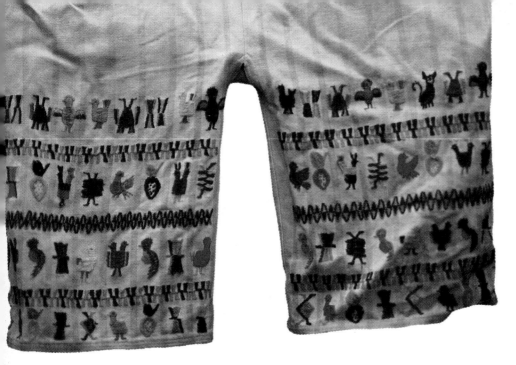

Maria's mother has embroidered colorful fruits, birds, and other objects on this pair of trousers.

An Ancient Art

Weaving is a skill that is valued in the community because each Indian village or town has a distinct style of clothing. Using a simple loom, Maria's mother creates nearly everything the family wears. She is a skilled weaver, and is now teaching Maria to weave. This is not an easy skill to learn, so Maria gets frustrated. But her mother knows that she will be a fine weaver, too.

Maria would rather spend the afternoons selling the family's handicraft to tourists passing on the street. The tourists, who come from all over the world, are always eager to buy her mother's weavings or the watercolors that she and Pedro create. Most of the visitors don't speak Spanish very well, and trying to communicate using gestures makes Maria giggle. She is glad that tourists are allowed to visit Santiago Atitlán. Because of the fighting in the countryside, the government sometimes restricts the areas that tourists can visit.

 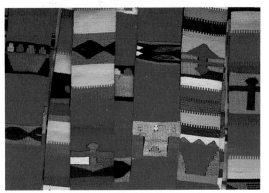

Top: Maria struggles with her weaving. Although she finds it frustrating, Maria hopes that she will learn to weave and embroider as beautifully as the pieces she sees at the orphanage.
Bottom left and right: Examples of typical Guatemalan embroidery and weaving.

Lake Atitlán's Colorful Markets

The family sells most of its produce and artwork at the market of Santiago Atitlán. People from five different villages travel to Santiago by foot, bus, and boat to buy and sell at this market. Maria and her mother go to the market almost every day. Like her mother, Maria carries her produce in a woven basket that she balances on her head. Girls learn to carry things this way at an early age. It takes much practice, and Maria is pleased to hear her mother remark on how skillful she has become.

At the market today, they sell the food that Pedro and Diego harvested late the day before. Their black beans and corn, which are the traditional foods of the Indian people, sell quickly. Most families eat corn tortillas and beans several times a day.

Maria and Pedro use a scale to weigh the beans that they will sell in the market.

Right: With bundles and baskets of produce, Maria and Pedro head for the market. Maria carries one bundle on her head.
Below: At the market, Maria sits on the ground and spreads the produce around her.

The market offers everything that the villagers eat, from grains and vegetables to fresh meat and fish. Besides food, the vendors also offer clothing, gardening tools, canned goods, and household supplies such as candles and soap. Most of the vendors are women. They display their goods in baskets or on mats that they arrange on the ground in front of them.

Across the lake, the regional market of Panajachel attracts Indians from all over Guatemala. When shopping there, Maria walks among the vendors, comparing prices and bargaining the way she has seen her mother do. She also studies women's clothing, trying to identify the different villages and towns. From her mother's teachings, Maria knows that each community's clothing is set apart by its particular patterns and colors. In the cities, Indian men have started wearing jeans, but in Santiago, most of them still wear the traditional embroidered pants, a Western-style shirt, and a cowboy hat.

Colorful patterns, such as those seen here, mark the traditional Guatemalan dress of each community.

Top: This pottery vendor, tending both her wares and her children, looks as though she'll be glad to see the day end.
Right: Another young vendor displays both the traditional dress of her people and her balancing skills.

Maria, Pedro, Diego — and Canela — travel across Lake Atitlán to gather firewood.
Maria and Pedro sit in the bottom of the canoe, which is lined with reeds. The reeds
keep them dry when water splashes over the sides.

A Canoe Trip across the Lake

The Reanda family often travels by canoe. Sometimes they
paddle all the way to San Pedro to visit relatives, but today,
Maria, Diego, and Pedro are going across the lake to collect
firewood. Maria can't wait to go because her father has said
she can paddle the canoe part of the way. She paddles standing
up, the way he has shown her. Paddling this way can be very
difficult, especially when it's windy and the waves are rough.

Left: Maria carries a bundle of firewood that is almost larger than she is.
Right: If Canela had known that a bath was part of the trip, she probably wouldn't have come along.

When they near the San Pedro volcano, they pull the canoe up on shore. Then they walk along the mountain paths, gathering branches and sticks. Maria and Pedro make a game of seeing who can balance the largest bundle of firewood. Afterward, Diego gives them a lesson on shooting accurately with a slingshot. By the time they're ready to return home, it's almost sunset.

42

Visiting the Temple of Maximón

Today, Maria, Pedro, and their parents pay their seasonal visit to the temple of Maximón, the traditional god of the Tzutuhil people. According to tradition, this god ensures good crops and weather, protects the people against invaders, and listens to their daily prayers. Because it is nearly time for planting, Maria, Pedro, and their parents will ask Maximón to bless the coming crops.

A religious group called the *confradía* cares for Maximón's temple. Before the Spaniards came to Santiago Atitlán, the confradía ruled the town. Even after the Spanish conquest introduced Christianity to the people, most of the Tzutuhils still considered the confradía their spiritual leaders. But they recognized the local Catholic priests as leaders, too. As many Tzutuhils do, Maria and her family honor both the God of Christianity and Maximón, the Mayan god.

The villagers adorn the statue of Maximón with colorful scarves.

◀ On a seasonal visit to the temple of Maximón, Maria, Diego, and Pedro pose with a statue of the god.

A Week of Celebration

Semana Santa, or Holy Week, is the most important religious festival of the year in Santiago Atitlán. It is Maria's favorite time of year, and she and her mother have been weaving new clothes, cooking special foods, and making final preparations for the holiday season for weeks.

Maria and Pedro have finished several new watercolors of Maximón as well as dozens of *cascarones*. Cascarones are empty eggshells that have been painted and filled with confetti. During the Easter celebration, it's customary to break the eggshell over a friend's head, spilling the colorful confetti. Maria reminds Pedro that this custom can also be used to show affection for another person. She wonders which boys will break an eggshell over her head.

Below: During Semana Santa, Maria and Pedro pay a special visit to the Catholic church that the family attends. Here they kneel before the church's main altar, which is surrounded by fresh flowers. Opposite page: Maria concentrates on decorating one of the cascarones.

Guatemalans celebrate Good Friday with a huge procession that winds through the streets carrying statues of Jesus (here in the casket) and Mary. A statue of Maximón, brought from his temple, joins the procession as a sign that he is considered equally important.

Beginning on Palm Sunday, which is the Sunday before Easter, and continuing for seven days, thousands of Tzutuhil villagers converge on the town. Maria and her family attend Mass, march in the colorful processions, and visit with friends and relatives. Schools are closed during this time, and most people stop working. A delightful sense of festivity takes hold. In the Reanda house there is much eating, drinking, and merriment.

During Holy Week, the Tzutuhils honor two deities: Jesus Christ of the Roman Catholic tradition and Maximón of the Mayan tradition. This week, they give thanks for the good things that have happened in the past year and pray for good fortune in the future. Like all other celebrations, Easter takes its place in the yearly cycle of planting and harvesting. After Easter, the rainy season begins, and this means that the new crops will soon grow. For Maria and all the people of Santiago Atitlán, then, Semana Santa is truly a time to celebrate.

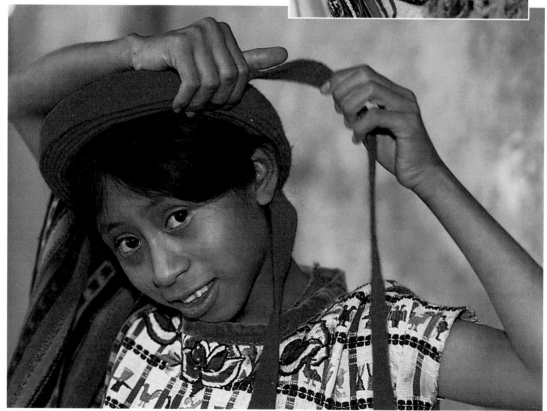

Right: The women of Santiago Atitlán join the procession, carrying candles shielded by banana leaves. Each wears a headdress, called a *cinta*, that is worn mainly for religious holidays.
Below: Maria shows how many yards of material are used to form the cinta.

FOR YOUR INFORMATION: Guatemala

Official name: Republica de Guatemala
(ray-POO-blee-kah deh wha-teh-MAH-lah)
Republic of Guatemala

Capital: Guatemala City

History

The Great Mayan Civilization

The Mayan Indians were the first people to live in what is now Guatemala.
Between 2500 BC and AD 1000, the Maya built a complex, sophisticated
civilization. At the peak of their history between AD 400 and 800, some
Maya inventions, such as their calendar or the use of zero in mathematics,
were more sophisticated than those of the advanced Greek and Roman
civilizations of the time.

One of the huge stone temples in the ancient Mayan city of Tikal —
a reminder of Guatemala's past.

The Maya studied astronomy, mathematics, and medicine. Their farmers were skilled, practicing an early form of soil conservation. By clearing only a small amount of land for crops and then growing a variety of plants, the Mayan farmers maintained the land's fertility. The Maya were also remarkable architects. Examples of their magnificent stone pyramids, temples, and sculptures still stand today. Many of these are found in the city of Tikal, once the religious and political center of the Mayan civilization.

For reasons that are still not totally clear, the Mayan civilization began to decline after AD 900. Factors such as disease, invasion, internal wars, and climate changes have been suggested as possible causes. Spanish conquistador Pedro de Alvarado conquered the Guatemalan Maya in 1523. The Maya were at first awed by the light-skinned Spaniards and their horses, but they soon saw that the Spaniards intended to take over their lands and enslave them.

The Spanish Colonial Period, 1523-1821

The Maya fought bravely against the Spanish invaders, but they were no match for the conquistadores. Unlike the Spaniards, the Maya had no guns, metal swords, armor, or horses with which to defend themselves. Hundreds of thousands of men, women, and children died at the hands of the Spanish invaders. Thousands more died of diseases that the conquistadores carried over from Europe. Many Maya committed suicide rather than submit to the Spanish tyranny. In 1524, for example, many Tzutuhils drowned themselves in Lake Atitlán rather than continue fighting against the Spanish invaders.

From 1523 to 1821, the Kingdom of Guatemala existed under Spanish control. This kingdom included land that now forms Guatemala, El Salvador, Honduras, Nicaragua, Costa Rica, and the modern Mexican state of Chiapas. Guatemala's ruling class, which included wealthy Spaniards, Ladinos (persons of mixed Indian and Spanish descent), and church leaders, exploited the Indian majority. These groups gained control of the best land, removed traditional tribal leaders, and tried to replace the native culture and religion. To manage the huge plantations that they had claimed for themselves, these new land-owners enslaved many of the Indians. Eventually, the Spaniards imported Africans to be used as slaves in Guatemala, too. While some landowners treated the Indian slaves decently, on the whole, the 300 years of Spanish rule brought the natives a miserable existence.

The Roman Catholic church became very wealthy and powerful in Guatemala. It owned huge sections of land and was heavily involved in farming and trade. In 1532, the church built Central America's first university in Guatemala. Named after Francisco Marroquín, Guatemala's first Catholic bishop, the university stood in the city of Antigua. Antigua, the second Spanish city built in Guatemala, succeeded Ciudad Vieja as the capital after Vieja was destroyed in an earth-quake. Antigua became the finest city in Central America, the home of artists, writers, sculptors, and craftsmen.

Over the years, Guatemala became the religious, cultural, and economic center of the Spanish colonies. The Spaniards exported crops such as rice, sugarcane, indigo (for blue dye), and cacao (for cocoa and chocolate), and increased the production of crops such as cotton and tobacco. They imported European fruits and vegetables as well as certain domesticated animals. These items all increased Spain's profit from its colony. But as the colony's trade grew, so did the restrictions placed on it. By law, the colony could trade only with Spain. Furthermore, certain items could not be produced because they would compete with the same products in Spain. These laws limiting the colonists' trade especially irritated merchants and landowners.

Independence, 1821-1944

By the early 19th century, Guatemalans grew ever more resentful of the Spanish authorities who ruled the colony and controlled their economy. About this time, the Spanish Empire began to decline because of wars with other European powers, as well as revolutions in its other New World colonies. On September 15, 1821, Guatemala declared independence from Spain for all the colonies of Central America.

No sooner had the colonies declared their independence than Mexican Emperor Agustín de Iturbide tried to force them to become part of his Mexican Empire. This empire lasted only a short time. When a revolution in Mexico overthrew Iturbide's government in 1823, the nations of Central America again declared independence. That year, these nations, which included Guatemala, El Salvador, Honduras, Nicaragua, and Costa Rica, formed the Central American Federation. Only Chiapas remained part of Mexico.

A year later, representatives from each of the federation's countries gathered in Guatemala City. There, they abolished slavery and wrote a constitution based upon that of the United States. But the changes the constitution brought about did not benefit the population's Indian majority. Instead, many of the changes, including the right to vote and freedom of religion, helped mainly those who owned land. Political differences finally split the federation in the late 1830s, and member countries turned their attention to individual growth.

Guatemala's early years as an independent nation were chaotic ones. As in most Central American countries, power struggles continued in Guatemala, mainly between two groups known loosely as the Liberals and the Conservatives. Church leaders and wealthy landowners made up the

Conservatives, while the Liberal party consisted mainly of merchants and the middle class.

A revolution in 1871 brought a Liberal, Justo Rufino Barrios, to power. As president, Barrios encouraged the country's economic development by increasing the production of certain crops, such as coffee, sugar, and cotton. He also reduced the power of the Catholic church in Guatemala by confiscating church lands and selling them, as well as by expelling many religious leaders. Barrios stressed education for all children and wanted to make it law that children attend school from the ages of 6 to 14. Unfortunately, Barrios was unable to complete that dream. He was killed in battle in El Salvador, while attempting to reestablish the Central American Federation.

Although Barrios had governed in an increasingly dictatorial way, he had attempted to modernize the country through his reforms. A string of leaders followed Barrios, but none seemed able to move the country farther forward. In some cases, it seemed to be moving backward. Powerful coffee growers seized the lands of Indians and small farmers. Economic privileges for the rich were restored and even strengthened. Political freedom and economic opportunities decreased. The situation for the Indians and the poor remained much the same as it had been under the Spaniards.

Guatemala's Democratic Revolution, 1944-54

In 1944, a Liberal group made up of Indians and middle-class Ladinos revolted, toppling the government. A new constitution went into effect, elections were held, and Juan José Arévalo became president. Arévalo's government forced the landowners to begin paying taxes on their landholdings and their business profits. The government also turned over to the Indians and poor Ladinos those lands that had been acquired illegally or were not being farmed. Through changes such as these, the new government forced people to respect the rights of the laborers and the Indians. For the first time in Guatemala's history, all citizens enjoyed the same rights. Between 1944 and 1954, Guatemala enjoyed a democratic and peaceful system of government.

Such reforms did not please everyone, especially the conservatives in the military and the powerful businessmen who didn't want to pay taxes or share their land or business profits with the workers. In 1954, Colonel Carlos Castillo Armas over-threw President Jacobo Arbenz Guzmán. A military dictatorship took power with the backing of the US government, which was protecting the investments of some US businesses. Castillo Armas destroyed many of the changes that had taken place in the last ten years. He abolished constitutional rights and banned all political opposition. He took back land that had been given to the peasants and returned it to the major landowners. Furthermore, he tortured, jailed, and killed anyone who opposed him. Over 30,000 Guatemalans died because of Castillo Armas's harsh policies.

Guatemala in Turmoil

Since the military coup of 1954, Guatemala has endured years of military and civilian dictatorships. Political violence has raged in the country almost since that time, with the military on one side and various rebel groups on the other. In 1982, the leading rebel groups united, forming the Guatemalan National Revolutionary Unity, or URNG. Recently, there has been increasing international pressure for the government and the URNG to end the fighting. But already, over 150,000 Mayan Indians and Ladinos have been murdered or kidnapped, while one million more have been removed from their homes. Such harsh treatment has quieted even peaceful efforts toward change, and much political opposition has gone underground, that is, opposition movements work in secret. According to human rights organizations such as the Americas Watch Committee and church-based monitors, since 1954, living conditions for the Indians and the poor in Guatemala are the worst in the Western Hemisphere.

In 1986, the people elected a civilian government for Guatemala, headed by Vinicio Cerezo Arévalo. At first, many people hoped that Cerezo's presidency would bring peace and change. Unfortunately, it has not. Repression of the Mayan Indian majority, in particular, continues to be one of the country's major problems. Although the government maintains that conditions inside the country are improving, human rights violations, including murders and kidnappings, continue to occur on a massive scale.

Government

According to its 1986 constitution, Guatemala is a republic that includes 22 departments, or states. Under the constitution, legislative power is held by the National Congress, whose 100 members serve five-year terms. In addition, each department has an elected governor; cities and towns have elected councils. These local governments, however, have very little power in comparison to the national government. Finally, although Indians make up the majority of the country's population, very few serve in the government.

The head of the government, according to the constitution, is the president, who is also elected for a five-year term. In reality, however, the constitution's democratic framework is often ignored. For most of the 20th century, the army has unofficially ruled the country. When the president or the National Congress tries to do something which the military doesn't approve of, the army usually threatens to overthrow the government. This has happened regularly since

1954. In 1988, and again in 1989, military factions tried to overthrow the president but failed. To keep the military from taking further action, the government then canceled planned social and economic reforms.

The Supreme Court of Justice heads the judicial branch of the government. It is composed of seven judges designated by the National Congress for a term of four years. Human rights organizations have repeatedly pointed out that no government or military official accused of human rights violations has ever been brought to trial by the Guatemalan judicial system. Yet these organizations have recorded at least 150,000 politically related murders and kidnappings since 1954. In 1985, the government passed a law that forbids putting military and police officers on trial for human rights violations. President Cerezo has all but admitted that he would be overthrown if he tried to bring military officials to trial for massacres or kidnappings.

Population and Ethnic Groups

After the arrival of the Spaniards, Guatemalans gradually became a people of both Spanish and Indian blood. By 1989, Guatemala's rapidly growing population had risen to approximately 9,000,000. Two distinct ethnic groups compose the majority of the population: Mayan Indian, 55%; Ladino (a mixture of Indian and Spanish blood), 42%. Pure whites and blacks make up the remaining 3% of the population.

Many pure-blooded Indians still live in the remote jungles or mountainous areas. As a result, an exact population figure is not available for them. Among these Indians and the poor, the average family has six children, but a high death rate for children usually reduces this number to five.

Religion

Many Guatemalans, especially the Indians, take religion very seriously. They attend church services regularly, and religious holidays mark major cultural events. Over 80% of the people belong to the Roman Catholic church; worship among the Indians is usually a mixture of Catholic and Mayan beliefs. The remainder of the population is mainly Protestant.

Despite the large Catholic population, very few priests and nuns serve Guatemala. Part of the reason for this is that the Catholic church was critical of the Guatemalan government in the early 1980s. The government claimed that the church was encouraging the Indians and the poor to revolt. In retaliation, hundreds of priests, nuns, and church workers were killed, causing other church leaders to flee the country.

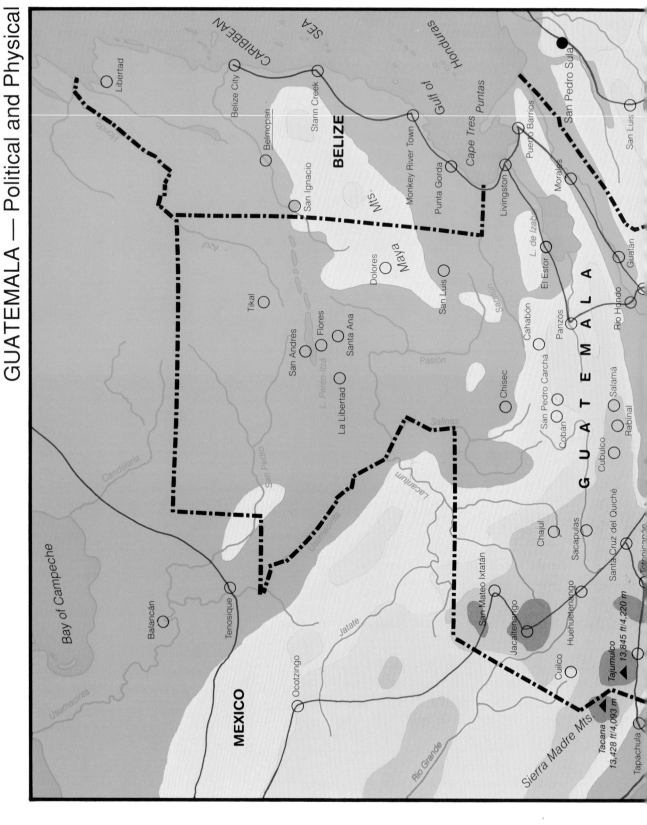

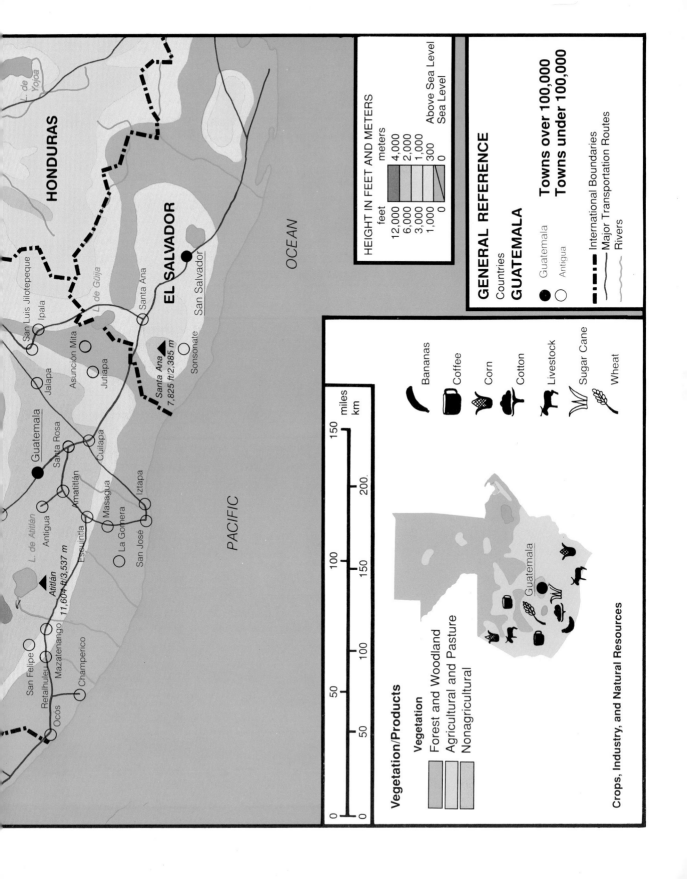

HONDURAS

L. de Yojoa

EL SALVADOR

San Salvador

Santa Ana

Sonsonate

Santa Ana
7,825 ft/2,385 m

San Luis Jilotepeque
Ipala
Asunción Mita
L. de Güija
Jutiapa
Jalapa
Guatemala
Santa Rosa
Amatitlán
Cuilapa
Antigua
Escuintla
Masagua
Iztapa
La Gomera
San José
L. de Atitlán
Atitlán
11,601 ft/3,537 m
San Felipe
Retalhuleu
Mazatenango
Champerico
Ocós

PACIFIC

OCEAN

HEIGHT IN FEET AND METERS

feet	meters
12,000	4,000
6,000	2,000
3,000	1,000
1,000	300
0	0

Above Sea Level
Sea Level

GENERAL REFERENCE

Countries
GUATEMALA

● Guatemala
○ Antigua

— · — International Boundaries
——— Major Transportation Routes
——— Rivers

Towns over 100,000
Towns under 100,000

Vegetation/Products

Vegetation
Forest and Woodland
Agricultural and Pasture
Nonagricultural

Bananas
Coffee
Corn
Cotton
Livestock
Sugar Cane
Wheat

Guatemala

Crops, Industry, and Natural Resources

miles
km

0   50   100   150

0   50   100   150   200   250

Land and Climate

Guatemala is the third largest country in Central America. It covers approximately 42,000 square miles (109,000 sq km) of land, which is about the size of the US state of Tennessee or twice the size of the Canadian province of Nova Scotia. Located in northwestern Central America, Guatemala is bordered by the countries of Mexico, Belize, Honduras, and El Salvador.

Guatemala has two basic types of terrain: the lowlands bordering the Pacific and the Caribbean coasts, and the central mountainous highlands, which make up about 50% of the country's total land area. The highlands are dotted with towering volcanoes, some of which are active. Currently, forests cover over 50% of the land, and another 26% is used for farming. Logging practices and cattle ranching have damaged these forests of fir, pine, willow, and oak trees.

Guatemala's largest lake, Lago de Izabal, is over 200 square miles (520 sq km) in size. Its highest mountain, Tajumulco, stands about 13,900 feet (4,200 m) above sea level. Earthquakes, which are common in the highlands, are often quite severe. A 1976 earthquake killed more than 20,000 people.

Guatemala is located in a tropical zone of the Western Hemisphere, but its temperate seas and mountainous landscape give it a wide range of climates. At sea level, average temperatures range between 77° and 86°F (25° to 30°C). In the higher elevations, average temperatures range as low as 55°F (13°C). Guatemala receives about 80 inches (2,030 mm) of rain annually. Most of it falls during the rainy season from May to November.

Natural Resources, Agriculture, and Industry

Because of its ample natural resources, Guatemala has the potential to be a wealthy country. But in many cases, the country's political and social problems take attention and money away from developing these resources. These problems also interfere with conservationists' efforts to preserve existing resources, such as the rain forests. Included among the country's resources are vast forest land, fertile soil (especially in the lowlands), and mineral deposits of petroleum, nickel, copper, zinc, iron ore, feldspar, and silver. Hydroelectric power provides a portion of the country's electricity, and the country, with its fast-flowing rivers, can develop this form of power even further. Other electricity is produced by oil-fired generators or is imported from neighboring countries.

Guatemala's economy relies on agriculture. Since the early 1980s, this industry has employed half the nation's work force. As in other Central American countries, many farmers run small family farms, where they grow Guatemala's

staple foods, such as corn and beans. Coffee, grown mainly on large plantations, has long been a critical export crop. The plantations also produce the
majority of the other major export crops, such as sugarcane, cotton, cattle, and
bananas. Most crops grow best on the lower mountain slopes or in the hot,
fertile lowlands, although corn grows well even at the higher elevations.

Guatemala also depends on its mines and factories, the most extensive in
Central America. Large deposits of nickel and oil already boost the country's
economy, and scientists suspect that they will discover more large oil deposits in
the future. Political fighting, however, is hampering oil exploration. Currently,
the country's main industries include food processing, rubber products, cloth
goods, paper products, and medical drugs. As Guatemala's main trading
partner, the United States buys approximately 30% of its exports and supplies
about 40% of its imports.

Guatemala's income and land taxes rank low among countries in the Western
Hemisphere. The country's national revenues come mainly from sales taxes
and import-export duties. These revenues, which support all government
activity, are small in comparison to the revenues of other Central American
countries. This lack of funding — as well as the ongoing political turmoil —
prevents Guatemala from fully developing its potential. Also, as in many other
countries, a small number of people control what wealth the country does
have. About 2% of the landowners, for example, control about 70% of the
agricultural land.   While many of the land and factory owners are wealthy,
most people who work for them are poor. Guatemala's society remains rigidly
divided into classes of rich and poor, although a middle class is growing.

Currency

The monetary unit in Guatemala is
the *quetzal*. As of September 1989,
one quetzal equaled 38 cents in US
currency. The currency gets its name
from Guatemala's national bird, the
quetzal, which is pictured on each bill.
Guatemalan coins come in units called
centavos. There are 100 centavos
to one quetzal.

Guatemalan paper money and coins.

Language

Spanish has long been the official language of Guatemala, but over 20 Mayan
languages are still spoken. The most widely spoken of these are Quiché,

Cakchiquel, Tzutuhil, Kekchí, and Pokom. Most Indians speak their own language as well as varying amounts of Spanish. People in remote villages speak very little Spanish.

Education

By law, Guatemalan children between the ages of 7 and 14 years must attend school. However, many Indian children must work full-time to help support their families. As a result, most are unable to complete more than a few years of elementary school, and only about 10% attend high school or college. Because of this, over half of Guatemala's people can neither read nor write. Although the government provides some money for education, classrooms in the rural areas are overcrowded, and teachers and schools are urgently needed.

Currently, over 60,000 students are studying at the university level in Guatemala. The largest university is the University of San Carlos in Guatemala City, founded in 1676. As at lower levels, college classes are overcrowded, textbooks are scarce and expensive, and facilities, equipment, and teachers are overworked and in short supply.

Art and Culture

Before the Spanish arrived in 1523, the Mayans had already mastered ceramics, sculpture, jewelry, weaving, and architecture. Guatemala has kept many of the original Indian traditions. Tourists, students, and archaeologists come in large numbers to explore the ancient Mayan pyramids, temples, and monuments in places like Tikal and Piedras Negras. Even today, rural Mayans build their houses in the traditional rectangle, with steep roofs made of thatch or corrugated iron. The Spanish used a style called Spanish Colonial in the construction of their public buildings and churches. This style features elaborately carved and decorated doorways, lofty domes, and arches on the outside of walls used as decorative forms. The deeply shadowed arches form a dramatic contrast with the light-colored building. Modern city structures often show the influence of this style.

But perhaps Guatemalans are most famous for their weaving. Weavers use cotton for their fabrics in the temperate and tropical areas, and wool in the colder regions. Intricate and colorful designs are unique to each area, and traditionally, people could read the colorful patterns on these fabrics like a book. They could learn the wearer's home, tribe, and language, among other things. People often decorate the clothing made from these fabrics with embroidery. In rural areas, nearly every woman becomes proficient using the backstrap loom. One end of this loom fastens to a post, and the other end attaches to a strap circling the weaver's back. On this loom, the woman weaves brightly colored fabric that she sells or uses to make her family's clothing.

Sports and Entertainment

Guatemalans play a variety of sports. The most popular sport is soccer, followed by basketball, which both girls and boys play. Most school grounds include a soccer field and a basketball court. Baseball, swimming, biking, and running also attract interest at many levels.

Among the Indian majority, religious festivals and holidays offer a chance for entertainment and relaxation. Very few rural towns have movie theaters, and many of the homes don't have television sets, so people in these areas tend to create their own forms of entertainment with story telling and simple games.

Guatemala City

With an estimated population of 1.8 million, Guatemala City is the largest city in Central America and the capital of Guatemala. It became Guatemala's

capital in 1776 after a severe earthquake devastated the former capital of Antigua. Guatemala City lies on a plateau of the Sierra Madre mountain range at an elevation of 4,900 feet (1,500 m). To its south stand a number of volcanoes, two of which are currently active. Earthquakes nearly destroyed the city in 1917-18 and then again in 1976. As a result, much colonial architecture was lost. So now, Guatemala City is a modern city, with cinemas, shopping centers, residential neighborhoods, and high-rise office buildings. While several neighborhoods are very wealthy, the majority are lower-income or poor neighborhoods. War refugees and victims of the 1976 earthquake live in some areas of extreme poverty.

This cathedral, known as Catedral Metropolitana, is found in Guatemala City's Central Park.

Guatemalans in North America

Because of Guatemala's political turmoil and economic problems, hundreds of thousands of Guatemalans have fled the country. Several hundred thousand are living in Mexico, 45,000 of them in refugee camps alone. Several hundred thousand more are living in the United States and Canada. Exact figures are difficult to obtain, because many Guatemalans have entered these countries illegally.

Almost all Guatemalan exiles claim that they are political refugees. In the United States, however, the Immigration and Naturalization Service has rejected over 95% of all Guatemalan requests for political asylum and has sent the refugees back to Guatemala. As a result of this situation, over 300 churches and synagogues in the United States have declared themselves "sanctuaries," offering to shelter these Guatemalan people. Although the Department of Justice arrested a number of these church activists for harboring illegal aliens, the groups continue to work toward resolving this situation.

Glossary of Useful Guatemalan (Spanish) Terms

adiós (ah-DYOS) .... goodbye
agua (AH-gwah) .... water
casa (CAH-sah) .... house
cascarones (cahs-kah-ROHN-ays) .... empty eggshells that are painted and filled with confetti as part of the Easter celebration
cayucos (kah-YOU-kohs) .... canoes
centavos (sen-TAH-vohs) .... Guatemalan coins
cinta (SEEN-tah) .... a headdress
confradía (cone-frah-DEE-ah) .... a special group of religious leaders
fincas (FINK-uhs) .... plantations
fuego (FWAY-goh) .... fire
Maximón (mah-she-MOHN) .... traditional god of the Tzutuhils
molino (moe-LEE-noh) .... corn grinder
patrones (pah-TRONE-ays) .... wealthy plantation owners
petates (pay-TAH-tays) .... mats made from reeds
quetzal (KATE-zal) .... the basic Guatemalan monetary unit
Semana Santa
    (seh-MAHN-ah SAHN-tah) .... Holy Week (the week before Easter)
tortilla (tor-TEE-yah) .... a round cake of cornmeal or wheat flour, often filled with meat or cheese
Tzutuhil (zoo-too-HEEL) .... one of the Mayan Indian tribes

More Books about Guatemala

Guatemala, a Country Study. Nyrop, editor (US Government Printing Office)
Guatemala in Pictures. Lerner Publications Dept. of Geography Staff (Lerner)
Hello Guatemala. Karen (Grosset & Dunlap)

Things to Do — Research Projects

The ethnic make-up of a country's people greatly influences its culture. Before the Spaniards came to Guatemala, for example, the country's population was made up of pure-blooded Mayan Indians. Since that time, Guatemala's population has gradually become a complex blend of Indian and Spanish heritage. Although full-blooded Indians still make up over half of the population, the Ladino population (the people of Indian-Spanish blood) grows larger every day. The effects of this mixture are seen in the country's economy, its religion, its politics, its arts, and in many other aspects of the everyday life of its people. The blend of the two cultures has created a third culture that gives Guatemala an interesting character all its own.

As you read about Guatemala, be aware of this blend and the way in which it affects life in that country — both past and present. Some of the research projects that follow require accurate, up-to-date information. That is why current newspapers and magazines are useful sources of information. Two publications your library may have will tell you about recent articles on many topics:

Readers' Guide to Periodical Literature
Children's Magazine Guide

Look up *Guatemala* in these two publications. They will lead you to the most up-to-date information you can find.

1. The sudden decline of the great Mayan cities in about AD 900 is still a mystery. Experts have not been able to identify exactly what led to this downfall. Try to learn more about the Mayan people. What do you think happened to the Mayan civilization?

2. In Santiago Atitlán, both men and women still wear traditional Guatemalan clothing. Look up the traditional Guatemalan clothing and draw a picture of what a man or a woman might wear today.

3. In Guatemala today, many Indians and poor Ladinos do not experience the same type of life that wealthier Guatemalans do. The Indians, especially, are a

group that is discriminated against. Read more about the conditions in present-day Guatemala. In what ways are the Indians and poor discriminated against?

More Things to Do — Activities

1. What aspect of Maria's life most interests you (such as school life, home life, or trips to the market)? Why?

2. The quetzal is Guatemala's national bird. Find out about this rare bird and what it looks like. Draw a picture of it.

3. As you have read, Guatemalan children sometimes have to drop out of school to help support their families. Imagine that you live in Guatemala and that your best friend has just told you that he or she is dropping out of school. Write to your friend listing reasons why he or she should stay in school.

4. If you would like to have a Guatemalan pen pal, write to these people:

International Pen Friends
P.O. Box 290065
Brooklyn, New York 11229

Worldwide Pen Friends
P.O. Box 39097
Downey, CA 90241

Be sure to tell them what country you want your pen pal to be from. Also include your full name, age, and address.

Maria calls, "¡Adiós!"

Index

This book may be kept
FOURTEEN DAYS
A fine will be charged for each
day the book is kept overtime.

OCT 0 3 1997		
DEC 1 1 1997		
MAY 26 1998		
APR 0 6 1999		
12/19		